Hygge. Huh?

A Little Book of Danish Bollocks

WILL MEADOWS

Published by FCD Publishing

First Published 2016

Copyright © Will Meadows 2016

ISBN: 1541004191
ISBN-13: 978-1541004191

PUBLISHER'S & AUTHOR'S DISCLAIMER

The material in this book is intended solely for informational purposes only. The majority of the content is a figment of the author's imagination. Any relationship to persons or places, real or imagined, is purely coincidental. There is little truth contained within these pages and the author's sole intention is to entertain and amuse. This is not a guidebook on how to live your life. If in doubt you should always consult a doctor and never trust an author. The author and publisher expressly disclaim any responsibility for any adverse effects that may result from the use or misuse of the information and advice contained within this book.

To the four most important people in my life:

My wonderful wife Jane

and my lovely children W, B & C.

I love you all. Thank you for crossing the World to be with me.

Thanks also to my good friend Henrik, for teaching me how to be Danish.

CONTENTS

1 INTRODUCTION

Hygge
(noun.) a complete absence of anything annoying or emotionally overwhelming; taking pleasure from the presence of gentle, soothing things.

Popular definition

"Hygge? It's that annoying Danish bollocks about wearing woolly socks and lighting candles isn't it?"

Will Meadows

In March 2016 *The World Happiness Report* was published. This report, compiled by the United Nation's Sustainable Development Solutions Network, seeks to list the World's happiest countries by surveying inhabitants and asking them to evaluate their lives on a scale of 1 to 10. Denmark was crowned the World's happiest country. The United Kingdom came in at a miserable 23rd place. What's more, Denmark took pole position again in 2010-2012 and has consistently scored in the top three since then. The UK meanwhile consistently languishes outside the top 20 with the United States just a few points ahead.

You might wonder why Denmark is so happy. Is a survey an adequate indicator of happiness? What if your national pride forces you to put on a brave face when asked questions about your state of happiness? What if the survey just happened to take place on a Sunday afternoon when most Danes are between their 'drinking to be merry' and 'drinking to fight like Vikings' modes? What would the result look like if you arrived during the 'fight like Vikings' timeslot? What does the British result say about us?

Not content with being happy, the Danes also lay claim to being one of the most equal societies on earth. Private education is heavily subsidised so even the best schools have a diverse student population from a variety of backgrounds. The social state and the trade unions are strong in Denmark. As a result the gap between rich and poor is smaller than experienced in other European nations. A street cleaner's salary might be half that of a lawyer. In other European nations they'd be lucky to earn 10%.

But what are these supposedly happy and equal people really like? Anyone who has ever met a Dane will tell you that they're more or less like anyone else. They get angry and they get happy just like we do. There is however a key difference which lies at the very heart of the Danish concept of 'hygge'. Whatever the Dane is doing, whether they are being happy or angry, they do it whilst wearing ridiculous knitted jumpers. This makes the Danes eternally festive. It's like Christmas every day in Denmark!

Jumpers aside, the Danes have many things to be proud of. They are a fiercely patriotic nation. They are proud of their Royal Family. They are proud of their country's achievements (don't mention the War). Danish inventors brought Lego and Ostomy bags to the world. They even stake a claim to the invention of the loudspeaker; albeit this was invented in the US, by a Danish born engineer and his American business partner.

If the conversation turns to sport the Danish will speak with animation about their national team's immense successes in disciplines that nobody really cares about: like Badminton. What's more, having bored you about their country's achievements in the 1996 Atlanta Olympics they'll ask bluntly (for they *are* a blunt nation) "Why is your country so shit at Badminton?". For the Danes, it seems their enthusiasm for the sport of badminton has made them blind to the rest of the World's indifference.

We spoke briefly about Danish technological inventions, but Denmark is also a land of farmers. The Danes sell a tremendous amount of pigs in the form of bacon. In fact they are amongst the World's major pig meat exporters producing around 28 Million pigs annually from 5,000 farms. 28 Million! That is 3.5 Million more pigs than there are Australians in Australia. If all Australians turned into pigs tomorrow then we'd be looking at a global bacon shortage. Thank God for Denmark! What's more, the Danish have mastered the skill of writing "Danish" in purple indelible ink on pigskin. This is important, as ink is an often-overlooked nutritional component that is missing from many people's diet [*citation needed*].

So far we have established that the Danes are happy, equal, patriotic, inventive, sporting and superb breeders (of pigs). With all these remarkable attributes it is perhaps no surprise that the Danish have gifted the world a concept that is centred on living the good life. A concept that has being comfortable at its very heart. This concept is known as hygge. But what is hygge?

Firstly, hygge is almost impossible to pronounce. It is variously explained as sounding like 'Heegee', 'Hoogah', 'Hugga' or 'Huggy'. It sounds like none of these. Even if you can make a noise that is approximately the same, a Dane will look at you like you're some kind of buffoon. They are simply not used to people trying to attempt to speak Danish so don't embarrass yourself trying. If you happen to meet anyone from Denmark (unlikely) then just spell out h-y-g-g-e. They should just about be able to understand what you mean. Denmark also boasts some of the World's highest educational standards amongst its other immense attributes.

Secondly, hygge is a word for which there is apparently no translation. I'm not entirely sure whether this is the case. People describe many things as being hygge: a walk in the park, a night by the fire, a meal with friends etc. The fact that the Danish haven't been bothered (too busy inventing etc) to create different words for these situations doesn't mean that hygge cannot be translated. It just means that it can be applied to many different situations. In English we might say we feel 'cozy' or 'comfortable' or 'content' or any word beginning with 'c'. The Danish just say hygge.

Unfortunately, the mystique surrounding this un-translatable word has given hygge a bit of a cult-like status. All over the world, the middle classes are lighting up[1] their dinner parties with talk of hygge, "I would absolutely *die* for a Klint Faaborg Chair. It's the essence of hygge and absolutely amazing!". Denmark and hygge has brought to the world conversations that anybody who is not a wanker would ever dream of having had before.

Whilst hygge may or may not be translatable, we have to wonder whether we, as non Danes, will ever be able to achieve a state of hygge. Having not had the opportunity to be born in the happiest place on earth, surrounded by equality, invention, knitwear and pigs. How can we ever reach a condition of such utter contentment to consider ourselves to be in a state of hygge? Is this zen-like state of mind in fact possible for us non-Danes?

This book is your guide to hygge, but without the bullshit. You will find no chapters on candles here. "Why! Oh Why?" you wail. This is why. You simply do not need to read about candles for 20 pages. You know what they are, you know where they go, how they work and what they do. Anyone who needs a book to tell them about candles has obviously been brought up by a pack of wolves. The only other explanation for needing to read 20 pages on candles is that you're a wanker. Which one is it? Wolf or wanker? Assuming you're neither, read on and explore hygge and learn why it isn't really all that different from what you're doing anyway[2].

---

[1] Quite literally 'lighting up'. Please see later.
[2] For those in a hurry, just buy some candles and a bottle of wine

2 THE DECEMBER HYGGE SEASON

"You may not have a handy light meter to take accurate measurements. So aim for at least five candles for that festive feeling – a survey found 31 percent of Danes light more than five candles at a time"

The Mail on Sunday

Any visitor to Copenhagen would likely have a bucket list of top attractions to see such as the Tivoli Gardens or The Little Mermaid. Imagine the thrill of wandering around this beautiful city catching glimpses of all these places you've only ever read about or seen on TV. It was therefore an odd decision for the *Lonely Planet Pocket Copenhagen Guide* to take when it recommended the 'feeling' of hygge as a highlight of any visit to the city.

In its endorsement of hygge, the *Lonely Planet* guide implores you to "grab a piece of the (hygge) action". So you don't miss out you're encouraged to visit Copenhagen in the winter. Hygge, it advises, reaches "fever pitch in December". During this month we are told the lights are twinkling and the mulled wine is flowing. It certainly seems like a magical place. We may lack the complex linguistic powers to be able to translate hygge however I'm going to have a go. Right here. Right now. I believe I have a word that more-or-less sums up this wonderful fairy-tale scene. That word is 'Christmas'. Coincidentally, 'Christmas' also takes place in December. At precisely the same time as the hygge high season.

You see, this is one of the problems we often encounter with hygge. Something happens that is generally quite nice. Like Christmas[3]. And the Danes then describe it as hygge and everyone with an inkling of new-age in their bones jumps on the bandwagon as though it's the secret to eternal happiness. It's not, it's just Christmas and for us non-Danes it's something we can enjoy without travelling to Copenhagen.

To make your Christmas hygge-like I would recommend

---

[3] Notwithstanding family arguments, eating too much and falling asleep in front of the Queen's speech.

installing a fake plastic or tinsel fir tree in the corner of your living room. This will bring a bit of the Scandinavian outdoors to your indoors. Once the tree is in place you will then need to decorate it. It's unlikely that you will be able to find any Copenhagen-style 'twinkling lights' to fit around this tree. After all, we're not Danish so such things might not be naturally available in our home country. However luckily the world is a small place and the artisan craftsmen of China produce a thing called 'Fairy Lights'. These provide a similar effect to Copenhagen's twinkling lights I am told. Time will tell if our own country's retailers will wake up to the hygge high season and start providing us with the equipment we need!

The second component of Christmas - I mean the hygge high season - is Mulled wine. This is known as gløgg in Denmark. Mulled wine, or gløgg , is vitally important for the attainment of hygge. Most of hygge is actually centred around getting drunk to the point *just before* you want to argue, fight and storm out of the room. Wine is a vital component of this as it delays the family flashpoint far more effectively than whisky; or cooking sherry.

To make a semi-decent tasting batch of mulled wine you will need:

Ingredients

An orange (available from most supermarkets),
150g caster sugar (likewise)
A bottle of red wine (If you don't know where to buy this, you'll never achieve hygge)
1 cinnamon stick (from all good cinnamon vendors) and;
5 cloves to stick into the orange (I've no idea who sells cloves. Try the Cinnamon man; or his wife Sally).

Method

1.   Stick all the above in a pan and heat gently.
2.   Pour into a glass whilst hoping that it doesn't shatter.
3.   Drink.
4.   Enter a state of hygge

That's it, perfect gløgg!

Alternatively you can just go to Tesco and get a bottle of their ready-made stuff. If you really want to become Scandinavian for a day, why not take a trip to Ikea? Ikea is from Sweden and they also sell mulled wine, although they call it *Glögg VinGlögg* just to be quirky. Incidentallly Sweden is the country the Danish visit to buy alcohol. They used to do 'booze cruises' but now there's a big long bridge that cuts down the journey time. Buying alcohol in Sweden enables the Danes to avoid paying alcohol duty. Why you'd want to travel to another country to avoid paying duty when everyone, including the street sweeper, is wealthy is beyond the realms of this book. Whilst you're in Ikea why don't you pick up a *behagfull* to stir your wine?

In this chapter we have discovered the most exciting time to visit Copenhagen, it is at the ~~peak hygge season~~ Christmas. We've also discovered how to make our homes look Scandinavian by employing some hygge design features: like a Christmas tree and some fairy lights. We've also discovered how to make a semi-decent batch of ~~glogg~~ mulled wine and shared some valuable effort-saving tips simply by utilising everyone's favourite Swedish flat pack furniture store.

In the next section we're going to explore how to hygge-up your life during those dark and cold winter nights.

Chapter Summary: Christmas

3 COLD WINTER NIGHTS

"Danish winters are long and dark, and so the Danes fight the darkness with their best weapon: hygge, and the millions of candles that go with it."

www.visitdenmark.com

One reason why hygge has gained in popularity is the popular belief that Denmark is such a miserable place to live. Not miserable in terms of quality of life. But miserable in terms of the winter climate and long winter nights. When you combine the notion of a miserable winter with the fact that the Danes frequently rate themselves as being the most insanely happy people in the World, then you've got a fad in the making.

It's true that winter can sometimes make life unpleasant. However I guarantee that you've never seen an unhappy Eskimo[4]. That's a fact. Nevertheless, for those keen to jump on the hygge happy-train there seems to be a startling paradox. How can the Danes possibly be happy when it's so cold and dark outside? It doesn't seem to make sense. Unless of course, the reason for all this happiness is hygge.

Now I struggle to understand what temperature and lumens have got to do with happiness. That said, I'm not one of those guys who sits at my desk next to a SAD[5] lamp (you know the type). Does temperature make you unhappy? I would suggest that anyone who has ever seen the *Ice Age* series of films will immediately recognise that hilarity can easily be achieved in the coldest of climates. That's an undisputable fact. As for darkness? There's a reason that comedy clubs are dimly lit. Enough said[6].

However, let's assume for just one minute that we accept that the dark and cold result in dire unhappiness. How can we use hygge to counterbalance nature's forces? I am now

---

[4] OK, Inuit.
[5] Seasonal Affective Disorder
[6] You will genuinely struggle to get a better scientific argument than this.

going to share a secret that only the Danes know. The Danes have a special way of combatting the cold; If it's cold outside you need to go *inside*. You see, it's warmer inside than it is outside. So you'll feel happier. Get it? No wonder you can't translate hygge – it's literally so complex that the English language couldn't possibly cope. You might think I'm being facetious, but this is actually part of many hygge self-help guides. If its cold outside, go inside where it's warm. Genius!

So let's assume you're inside. What should you do? We hinted at this earlier in the book. It has something to do with the provision of light; not the fairy lights, the other one. Still not got it? OK, to explain this I'm going to have to take you back to 1986 for the earliest non-Danish example of hygge ever caught on camera. It is of course the video to *Wham!'s* seminal chart topping hit *Last Christmas.* At precisely 2 minutes and 11 seconds into the song the *Wham!* boys are hosting a hygge-themed dinner party in a remote alpine chalet. We cannot help but notice the poor quality of lighting in the room despite the story of unrequited love unfolding before our squinting eyes. The source of this poor lighting? Candles!

Candles are one of the most absolutely amazing things about hygge. This is why some books devote whole chapters to the subject (see previous comments). Candles are amazing because they make you act in a counter intuitive manner. When confronted by darkness, a non-Dane would probably instinctively reach for the light switch. But that's not what the hygge-informed Danes do. The Danes will keep the lights off and instead opt for the inefficient and potentially dangerous lighting source that is the candle. How clever are they?

As if to hammer home the fact that the Danish have got it sussed when it comes to cold winter nights, another key component of the typical hygge scene is a crackling log fire. It seems that you can never be truly cozy without a raging fire in your living room. This might be why a news report in 2015 informed us that 360,000 Danes had experienced a fire at home during the previous five years[7]. If you don't have a log fire at home then, put simply, you will *never* be able to achieve a state of hygge. You will have failed to achieve cozyness. You should seriously consider moving home.

In this section we have learnt that humour can still exist in the cold and dark. We have also discovered that the best refuge from the cold outdoors is the warm indoors. Bringing naked flames into the picture by lighting candles and a fire will increase your happiness tenfold.

Chapter Summary: I'm a firestarter, twisted firestarter.

---

[7] http://cphpost.dk/news/over-a-quarter-of-all-danish-homes-dont-have-smoke-alarms.html

4 DINING WITH FRIENDS

"Champagne is not just for sipping on at elegant parties. Its refined taste can also be matched with food and, fits in nicely with the latest Danish trend of creating a cosy atmosphere in winter"

Moet & Chandon feature in *The Independent*

The Danish are sociable people. Spending time with friends is very hygge[8]. In fact many books and articles devote a lot of time to this topic. In advising you to spend time with friends there is a tacit assumption that the rest of the world is an unfriendly place that really needs to cotton on to friendship groups. Luckily the Danes are here to explain the concept of 'friends' to us. To make the World a better place.

One of the ways in which the Danes work to make the World a better place is by *dining with friends*. It goes without saying that in most countries outside of Denmark the dinner party will consist of a bunch of strangers the hosts have never met before. These guests will have typically been plucked randomly from the street a few moments before the main dish comes out of the oven. This can often make the whole process a tad uncomfortable. Particularly if one of the guests doesn't eat meat, or smells of wee. Luckily this book is here to help you navigate this minefield the Danish way.

Firstly, 'friends' does not include family. Family are a pain in the arse and no matter how much you're looking forward to seeing Uncle Bernie, he'll say something completely inappropriate and will later go on to upset your children. Worse still, you could invite your sister around and then spend the next day wondering why she didn't text you to say 'thank you'. You will start the day worrying that you'd somehow offended her and end the day raging about what a selfish bitch she really is[9]. Families eh?

---

[8] Did I really just write "Spending time with friends is very hygge"? I'm starting to use their words. I'm becoming one of *them*!

[9] Any relation to real sisters is purely coincidental

So, for a hygge-style dinner party to really work you should invite friends only. Real friends. Not those guys from work. Being a wealthy society where everyone including the street cleaner is minted you'd expect the Danes to host lavish parties with no limit on excess. However this is not the case. Often the host will serve up just one dish, or prepare some light snacks in advance to enjoy throughout the evening. The pretence of this is to give the host more time to spend with their friends. Another very popular method is to ask each guest to cook a meal and bring it to the party. You fucking what? Yes, Danish dinner parties are done on the cheap.

To be the perfect host and to create real hygge at home, all you need to do is provide a couple of serving spoons and some plates and wait for the guests to arrive laden down with the meals they have prepared for your party. Should you feel the need to contribute, you should offer to make some side dishes. A good scam is to contact each guest in advance and pretend to be really interested in what they are bringing. Tell them you want your side dishes to complement their offering. You can then basically ignore whatever they told you and follow the instructions below. This is guaranteed[10] to work for all occasions:

Ingredients

A small number of pre-prepared Microwavable Vegetable Side Dishes (available from most supermarkets)

---

[10] This is unlikely to work for all occasions.

Method

1. Cook in microwave as per instructions on packet sleeve.
2. Remove from microwave and remove film lid.
3. Tip into your own serving bowl and arrange the contents so they look homemade.
4. If serving mashed potato or mashed swede, make some wavy lines on the surface with a fork to make it look like you've followed a recipe.
5. For other vegetable dishes, add some meaningless garnish to create that 'home made' illusion. Thyme or mint is always a safe bet.
6. Take to the table.
7. Tell everyone you hope the food hasn't gone cold because you were so busy in the kitchen.
8. Soak up the praise.

This stunning hygge time saver not only works for vegetable sides, it's also excellent for desserts! Choose an impressive looking hot dessert from the microwave food aisle in your local supermarket. Follow the instructions above however instead of thyme/mint, you can substitute a couple of poncey berries like redcurrants - or the ones with the name that sounds like syphilis. For cold desserts, some citrus peel or chocolate shavings scattered about works a treat.

Obviously to really hit the hygge-spot you need to get the guests drunk. Typically your guests will bring a decent bottle of wine to the party so they don't look cheap. This is regardless of how much time and money they've spent cooking for you. There are plenty of apps that allow you to scan the barcodes of wines to enable you to determine if your guests are cheapskates. You should make your guests aware in advance that you will be scanning the wine on entry to ensure the quality of the provided beverages. Alternatively, you can scan the codes in secret and ensure that any truly decent bottles are held in reserve for your private enjoyment. Hygge might be about friends, but you've got to get something out of it as well. Right?

Chapter Summary: Prick and Ping

WILL MEADOWS

5 WINTER WALKS

"Walking outside in bad weather has a great hygge effect as that warm drink when you get home will feel so good"

Lifestyle website

We learnt in earlier chapters that the outside was a cold and foreboding place from which the only sanctuary was escaping inside and settling down next to a raging fire. Unfortunately the Danes realised that being unable to step outside is an occupation solely 'enjoyed' by agoraphobics. You simply *have* to go outside at some point. If only to buy more candles.

The hygge guide to the outdoors is not what we might usually experience. In non-Danish countries a venture into the outdoors typically means trudging in the pissing rain to the corner shop to buy toilet rolls because you've run out. This will generally involve a car speeding through a puddle to soak you through. When you arrive at the shop you will inevitably have to walk across soggy cardboard so you don't slip on the wet lino. This is the typical outdoor experience of everyone who does not live in Denmark. However our outdoor experience is the antithesis of hygge. It is the anti-hygge.

For the Danes, a trip to the outdoors will not normally involve toilet rolls or soggy cardboard[11]. In Denmark, your outdoor experience is likely to involve throwing a picnic blanket down on a mossy hillside. From there you will lie on the ground gazing at the stars whilst your companions pour a mug of delicious hot chocolate. Later you will sit around a crackling campfire whilst shadows dance around the hillside. You will share anecdotes and laugh and joke with your companions. The mug of hot chocolate bringing a welcoming warmth to your cupped hands. You will later return home to the comfort of your candlelit bedroom and smile as you drift off to sleep. High from the friendship and fresh air. This is of course complete and utter bollocks. Who does this stuff? Not you or I for sure.

---

[11] With the exception of certain specialist gentlemen's clubs

You are never going to walk up a hillside in the dark with a flask of hot chocolate. Never in a million years. Don't even think about it. You don't live in Denmark. Instead you need to try to adapt the hygge outdoor experience to your own environment. You might for example want to 'walk to the pub'. If the pub has an open fire, then you've got hygge sorted without the hassle of cleaning the grate. If you feel that you want to get closer to nature, why don't you 'visit the garden centre'? Here you can enjoy Danish-style cups of hot chocolate whilst perusing their range of reasonably priced hygge Christmas decorations (see earlier chapter).

In this section we have learnt that yet another part of the hygge concept is based on an overly romanticised version of reality. You are highly unlikely, at your age, to change your ways. So why bother trying? Instead go to the pub. No matter where you live, unless you live in a pub, you'll need to go outdoors to get there. Hygge. Sorted.

Chapter Summary: Avoid the countryside. It's not for you.

6 MUSIC TO HYGGE TO

"Danish Music: Great music to listen to if you don't want people to know what you're listening to"

Top definition: urbandictionary.com

It's cold and dark outside but you're in the warmth. The candles are lit and you're relaxing with a loved one in front of a raging log fire three bar electric fire. Now it's time to make that mood that little bit more relaxing. You slide over to the Hi-Fi (that's how old I am) and put on a CD (again, that's how old I am) of your favourite tracks. This is music for hygge-ing.

Some hygge Consultants (unfortunately that really is a thing) suggest chilling to the likes of Norah Jones, Rufus Wainwright or maybe a bit of Annie Lennox. So basically they want your house to sound like the local branch of Poundstretcher. What self-respecting Dane would ever listen to these artists? My guess is the hygge consultants chose these songsters because there's never been a famous Danish band (with the obvious exceptions of *De Nattergale* and *Efterklang*).

My suggestion would be to stick with what you know. Even if what you know is Megadeth or Metallica, or indeed any band beginning with 'M'. With the exception of Mumford and Sons for obvious reasons. The hygge power of the candle will be enough to mellow your mood. It is no coincidence that when cigarette lighters are held aloft in vast concert halls the music gets mellower. The hygge force is strong.

Chapter Summary: Kenny G

7 CLOTHING

"Hygge slippers, inspired by the woven baskets that children in Scandinavia make to fill with sweets and hang on the Christmas tree"

Product Description

I grew up at a time when everyone had an Uncle who was a bit of a 'ladies man'. Families that lacked a real Uncle didn't lose out. In those innocent days any male neighbour or friend of the family was called Uncle. The more married he was, the more of a ladies man he had the potential to become. It was the era of drink driving, sexist comedies on TV and frequent power cuts. It was the best of times, it was the worst of times.

Part of the charm of these Uncles was that they *knew* how to talk to 'the ladies'. Not for them was the thrill of the wolf whistle. Whilst other, lesser men, would be screaming sexual innuendo at their prey, these Uncles would sidle up and offer to 'share a fag[12]' with the lady. They were smooth operators.

These ladies men shared a few key identifying factors. One was a luxurious mane of slicked back hair. Brylcreem being the male grooming product of choice. The second factor was the latest digital watch. Invariably this was something gold coloured with a little button on the side so you could tell the time in the dark. The last factor, common to all ladies men – was the sweater! After the hair, this was the next thing their new lady friend would notice across a crowded working men's club. Once the hair and sweater had pulled them in, the gold Casio would blow them away. Bingo! Legs eleven.

So what has this to do with hygge? Any self-respecting book on hygge will mention clothing at some point. This may be alongside a statement about hygge being a 'feeling' and definitely not about material things (see chapter on candles and wine). Nevertheless there will be a suggestion that to achieve the peak of hygge-ness you need to enter the material world[13]. To do this, you will need to invest in

---

[12] The term 'fag' related solely to cigarettes in those days.

a woolly jumper. And so it was, in an apparent insult to all the Uncles of my youth, that the Danish chose to claim the sweater as their own. But what does hygge fashion look like?

If you do a Google search of hygge fashion you will inevitably come across a picture of someone wearing what can only be described as a 'Christmas Jumper'. You know, the type of jumper you wear for a laugh at the office Christmas party because it's so shit. Now, imagine someone wearing such a jumper who isn't having a laugh at the office Christmas party. Instead this person is sat in a dark room in front of a flickering candle. Maybe there's a pickled gherkin on the plate next to them? You've just conjured up an image of a hygge in full force. Miserable or not, these guys are at the forefront of hygge fashion. But how do you get that look?

In the phenomenally successful Danish TV Series, *The Killing*, the main character Sarah Lund wears the most awful jumper ever created. Despite wandering around in the bleakest weather imaginable and looking miserable for most of the series, Lund is hygge in human form. Outside she may seem miserable but inside she's cozy as fuck. The key to her state of hygge was the jumper. In fact, the Lund sweater got so much press that supermodels such as Helena Christensen took to wearing it in an ironic 'look at me, I'm dressed like shit but I look beautiful, crazy eh?' sort of way.

If you want the hygge look you can buy a copy of the original jumper online. These jumpers are hand knitted in Greenland, a Danish administrative region. The cost of this iconic piece of knitwear is a little bit over 300 Euros. Alternatively, an ebay search for 'tacky Christmas jumper'

---

[13] Copyright Madonna

will threw up a near identical jumper (albeit with 'Ho,Ho,Ho' written across the front) with a 'Buy it Now' price of only £9.99.

In this section we have learnt that fashion is not everything. This is especially true to achieve hygge. The main aim is to be comfortable and to not give a toss about what you look like. You can always claim you were being ironic later.

Chapter Summary: In the old days men who were slightly less sexist than other men appeared to be more attractive. To get that look today, go to ebay.

8 HOME FURNISHINGS

"Lighting plays a vital role in hygge with Danes opting for lamps and candles over large ceiling lights. As such, fireplaces are key to embracing hygge and Scotland boasts a wealth of cosy pubs with open fireplaces – very hygge"

Visit Scotland Promotion in *The Scotsman*

It's a cold winter night in late December and you've escaped the dark and cold to the warmth of your home. Maybe you're going to be entertaining friends, or relaxing to some hygge inspired tunes? To create the right ambience you're probably going to need some top quality interior design tips. Unfortunately you've ended up with this book. Not to worry, below is all you need to know about hygge inspired interior design. Anything more is just fluff and filler. Read on.

Lighting is the key to the hygge home. We've previously mentioned the powerful allure of the candle. However only an idiot, or a squatter, would use only candles in their homes. You need to supplement your candles with subtle and understated lamps to create a soft warm glow. This is somewhat akin to not leaving the 'big light'[14] on. Can you believe you need a book to tell you that? Not only that, a book that recommends you kit out your house like some dude from Jutland. Are you mad?

Assuming you're not mad and are genuinely interested in Scandinavian design, there's a lot you can do to hygge up your home. Something the Danish are particularly fond of is, wait for it, blankets and pillows. Not only that, they use them on beds! To create the hygge effect in the bedroom simply put pillows on your bed, and a blanket. This will not only provide a resting place for your head, but also warmth in the night (see earlier chapter on cold).

Denmark is famous for its designers. In fact, Denmark is famous for dead designers. In their lifetime these designers made very famous chairs. These chairs have been produced, unchanged, for the last 100 years or so. Modern Danish designers have struggled to compete with their dead ancestors so you will be unlikely to find anything

---

[14] Northern English slang for the main light in a room

stylish that is Danish that isn't decades old. In the hygge home these ancient chairs are used to sit on. Maybe whilst enjoying a meal with people you actually know, or whilst removing your hot chocolate stained boots after a ramble in the countryside. No matter for what purpose you believer you require a chair, no hygge home is complete without something to sit on.

You might have guessed from the home furnishing recommendations above that information on hygge design is scant; and you'd be right. In fact, because hygge is really about feeling cozy all you need to do is kit out your house in things that create that feeling for *you*. There's no need to follow a guidebook – even though there are plenty to choose from! If you don't know what makes you feel comfortable, how do you expect anyone else to be able to tell you?

OK, I guess you're still not convinced and need some creative design tips? Luckily you don't need to trawl through numerous hygge books, magazine articles and websites because I have done all the work for you! Please find below, in strict order of importance, the ultimate hygge interior design guide:

1. Candles (who would have thought it?)
2. A real fireplace or log burner
3. Cushions, throws and blankets
4. Subtle lighting and lamps
5. Simple furniture. Preferably wooden. Preferably Danish.
6. Pale wall colours
7. Photos and pictures
8. Wooden floors
9. Natural day light

That's it! Hygge for the home. There's no more to know.

Please don't try to make your home look Danish. You'll fail. Make your home look comfortable for you. There is no big secret to this.

Chapter summary: Ikea

9 CONCLUSION: THE DANISH MENTAL STATE

"38% of Danish women and 32% of Danish men will receive professional treatment for a mental disorder at some point during their lifetime"

Findings from *A Comprehensive Nationwide Study of the Incidence Rate and Lifetime Risk for Treated Mental Disorders*
JAMA May 2014

I have poked fun at the concept of hygge throughout this short book. It's not the concept of hygge per se that I find funny. It's the bandwagon that has sprung up around it. It's the earnestness of the people trying to tell us to wear a jumper when it's cold that I find hilarious. I hope you do too. However there is one aspect of hygge that overrides all the others and I have saved it for the end of the book. It is the concept of happiness.

You may have read the startling fact on the previous page. If you skimmed over it, go back and read it now. What this fact tells us is that over a *third* of all Danish men and women have received professional treatment for a mental disorder at some stage in their life. Think carefully about this. Over a *third* have sought out *professional medical help* for their mental state. How many others didn't seek help and suffered in silence, or worse? This fact, and it is a bona fide fact, is in stark contrast to the image of the happiest nation on earth.

When I first discovered this survey into the nation's mental health I didn't really know what to think. How come these people didn't get to fill in the happiness survey? What would we be saying about Denmark today if the reality of widespread mental disorder were more widely known? Would we all be clamouring to copy a nation where a significant proportion of the population is battling with terrible mental issues?

Here's another fact. The happiness survey's sample size was in the region of 1,000 people. Only 1,000 people filled in the survey questionnaire. This amounts to around 0.017% of the Danish population. This is the basis on which Denmark has been consistently crowned the happiest nation in the World over successive years. In stark contrast, the study into mental disorder sampled *all* Danish residents: 100%, 5.6 *million* people. What's more, the study was conducted over a 13-year period. Which survey do you think is the most accurate? The study where 1,000 people were asked if they were happy one afternoon, or the study where 5.6 million people had their medical records checked for over a decade?

So what can we learn from this? It's clear that appearances are often only skin deep. We might try to imitate the Danish by lighting up candles and wearing thick socks. However all we're doing is copying what someone else does and hoping it can make us feel as happy as we believe they are. Instead why don't we just try to be comfortable with who we are, what we have and try to be happy in our own skin? Spending time with our friends and trying to create a little bit of comfort in our own surroundings can work wonders. If you don't have the money to kit out your whole house, just create a little corner where you can relax. Our life may not be perfect but a positive outlook and close friendships can achieve far more than an ugly jumper or a new pair of socks. If however those socks are your route to achieving contentment, then who am I to say?

Chapter summary: Give yourself a big hygge.

Will Meadows
Shanghai
Winter 2016

ABOUT THE AUTHOR

Will Meadows was born and grew up in a once-proud South Yorkshire town. Much of his working life has been spent travelling the globe and he has a particular fondness for Asia.

His career has spanned a number of industries with the majority of his experience in the fields of diet and nutrition.

Will has authored a number of magazine and journal articles. A distillation of Will's personal and working experiences can be found in *The Final Countdown Diet* and other titles such as the 2015 edition of *The Banting Diet: Letter on Corpulence.*

He currently lives in Shanghai with his wife Jane and their three children. He often travels back to Yorkshire to sit by the fire in his local pub with a pint of IPA in his hand. Will doesn't have a special term for the feeling he gets when he does this. He simply calls it 'going to the pub'. Will has more than one Danish friend but fewer than five.

Printed in Great Britain
by Amazon